Ramses II, pharaoh of the nineteenth dynasty

The FIRST BOOK of

ANCIENT EGYPT

by

Charles Alexander Robinson, Jr.

Pictures by Lili Réthi

FRANKLIN WATTS | NEW YORK | LONDON

For my grandchildren

15 16 17 18 19 20

Library of Congress Catalog Card Number: 61-5201
© 1961 by Franklin Watts, Inc.
Printed in the United States of America

SBN 531-00462-7

Contents

Temple of Queen Hatshepsut, daughter of Thutmose I, at Thebes

Egypt and the River Nile

IN A VERY REAL SENSE Egypt and the River Nile are one. If it were not for the Nile, all Egypt would be a desert. This life-giving stream rises in Central Africa and the mountains of Ethiopia. It flows several hundred miles to Aswan, or Assuan, the ancient Syene, where today the Egyptians are building a large dam. This is the site of the first of six rapids, or cataracts, that the traveler meets on his journey up the Nile from its mouth.

From Aswan the Nile continues six hundred miles to Cairo, where the ancient city of Memphis stood. Throughout the whole of this distance the river flows between limestone hills in a valley only ten to thirty miles wide. In ancient times this area, from Syene almost as far as Memphis, was called Upper Egypt.

At Cairo the hills disappear, and the Nile flows for a hundred miles through flat and marshy land to empty, by several channels, into the Mediterranean Sea. This part of the country was once called Lower Egypt. It is often called the Delta because its triangular shape resembles the fourth letter of the Greek alphabet.

The Nile is the longest river in Africa and the Nile river system is the longest in the world. But the most remarkable thing about it is that every summer the monsoons, or tropical rains, in Ethiopia cause it to rise and overflow its banks and flood the land. Everything beyond the reach of the overflow is desert, but as the water

1

returns to its channel in December, it leaves a rich deposit of earth, or silt, on the land it covered. This silt so fertilizes the ground that a man can raise a couple of crops a year on it providing — and here is the important part — he continues to irrigate it.

The Rise of Civilization

IT IS a strange but simple fact that civilization began where men had to irrigate the land in order to grow food and where, from time to time, they were overwhelmed by floods. Mesopotamia, the valley between the Tigris and Euphrates Rivers, was such a place, and so was the valley of the Indus River in northern India. The valley of the Nile was another.

In order to irrigate his land, the farmer of ancient Egypt had to lift water out of the Nile or out of wells and send it across his fields through a complex system of canals. The Nile's rise is normally about twenty feet, but in some years it might be very small, bringing famine to the country. Another year it might bring a flood that destroyed canals and even villages. Therefore, the Egyptians had to learn very early how to control the floods and store up water if they were going to live on the land at all. No man could do the job alone. All the people had to work together.

When a great many people work together, there must be leaders to help plan and direct the work. In short, there must be government. And when people live and work together under a central

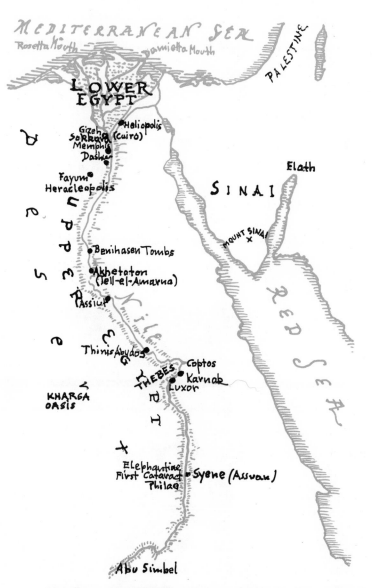

MEDITERRANEAN SEA
Rosetta Mouth
Damietta Mouth
PALESTINE

LOWER EGYPT

•Heliopolis
Gizeh• (Cairo)
Sakkara•
Memphis•
Dashur•

Fayum•
Heracleopolis

•Benihasen Tombs
Akhetaton•
(Tell-el-Amarna)

•Assiut

Thinis•Abydos

THEBES
Coptos•
•Karnak
Luxor•

KHARGA
OASIS

Elephantine
First Cataract •Syene (Assuan)
Philae

Abu Simbel

SINAI

Elath

MOUNT SINAI
x

RED SEA

UPPER EGYPT

Nile

ANCIENT EGYPT

government, they soon begin to build cities, to manufacture things, to trade with their neighbors and people far away. This is what happened in Egypt.

Another reason why civilization grew so rapidly in Egypt was that the Egyptians were all crowded together in their narrow valley. When people live this way, they have to compete with each other, they exchange ideas, and become more curious.

Before 3000 B.C. the Egyptians not only had a government and lived in cities, but they also used metals and had learned to write. They still shaped their pottery by hand, but soon learned to shape it on a crude, horizontal wheel — actually a turntable. This was the first potter's wheel, and it was a truly important invention. Now people could make their cups and dishes more quickly and,

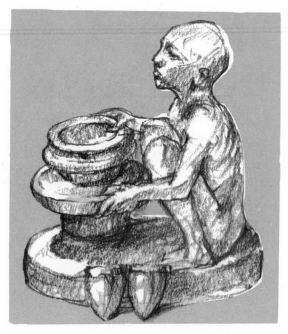

A potter and his wheel.
(Limestone sculpture,
2600-2400 B.C.)

4

if they had any eye at all for line and design, they were challenged to turn out beautiful objects.

Once the Egyptians discovered how to work metals — particularly how to mix tin and copper to make bronze — they were able to make far better implements than the stone ones they had used before. But what was even more important, this new knowledge stirred their imaginations. One new invention led to another.

The Egyptians taught themselves to write when government and trade grew so big and complicated that they had to find some way to keep records. They developed an alphabet, and used pictures called *hieroglyphs* to represent the letters. They drew these little picture-letters with reed pens and brushes dipped in red and black ink made of gum and colored earth.

A scribe of the Old Kingdom. This limestone figure, painted red, is in the Louvre, Paris.

The writing paper the Egyptians invented was used throughout most of the ancient world. It was made by pressing together flat strips cut from the stalks of the papyrus plant, which grew everywhere in the Egyptian marshes. Since these strips were usually very long, the Egyptians rolled their writing paper into cylinders when they were not using it.

For a long time the Egyptians had a lunar calendar — that is, a calendar measured by the moon's revolutions. It gave them months of twenty-eight days each. Then, about 2850 B.C., they worked out their civil, or state, calendar of 365 days a year.

When we think of the backwardness of Greece and Rome and western Europe in the first centuries after 3000 B.C., Egyptian civilization seems breathtaking. Nowhere, during all of ancient times, did men construct such tremendous buildings as they did in Egypt. Nowhere today do the monuments of the past stand in such large numbers. Nowhere are they so well preserved. When we think of Egypt, we quite naturally think of pyramids and obelisks and temples, of statues and paintings. But those are not all that remain of that ancient civilization. There are also great quantities of papyri, the first writing paper, which have been preserved by the dry climate.

All this means that we know a good deal about ancient Egypt, including many of the details of daily life. For example, we can follow the course of a law suit over many years. The record is there for us to read on the ancient paper. We can watch an Egyptian go to the post office and register a letter, and then we can watch the letter being carried up the Nile to be signed for by an official, and finally by the person to whom it is addressed. We have the receipts, and also the letter itself.

The civilization that the Egyptians developed was among the greatest in the history of the world. In time, fortunately, the ways of civilization spread to Palestine, Greece, and Rome, where our own European civilization began.

Earliest Egypt

DURING the Paleolithic (Old Stone) Age, men in Egypt and everywhere else were pretty much at the mercy of nature. They ate wild berries and roots and the flesh of wild animals. They had no permanent dwellings. Slowly, however, they learned to make stone tools, to grow crops, and to herd animals. Life, though still not civilized, was pleasant in comparison to what it had been.

It was during this new period — known as the Neolithic (New Stone) Age — that Libyans came to Egypt from the northwest, Semites from the northeast, and Negroes from the south. These were the early ancestors of the Egyptian people.

Men now lived in huts of mud bricks or mud and reeds. They worshiped spirits and placed objects of daily use into the graves of the dead. The vases, the flint tools, and sculptured figures were often very beautiful.

But life was simple, and the people were scattered in villages.

HOW THE EGYPTIANS LEARNED TO BUILD

A wooden house made of planks tied together with ropes.

(About 3000 B.C.)

A crude shelter of palm sticks woven into a screen.
(About 4000 B.C., or earlier.)

Hut made of reeds plastered with mud.
(About 3500 B.C.)

A brick house with two bins for storing corn. (About 1200 B.C.)

It was when the Egyptians began to build cities and develop other ways of civilization that their greatest period of history began. It lasted for two thousand years.

In the third century before Christ, an Egyptian named Manetho divided the history of his country into periods of time, which he called the Old, Middle, and New Kingdoms. Each of these covered the rule of several dynasties, or families, of kings.

8

The Old Kingdom (2780-2280 B.C.)

EARLY EGYPT was divided into two kingdoms — Upper, and Lower Egypt. Then, not long after 3000 B.C., a powerful king called Menes united the two kingdoms and set up his capital at Memphis in Lower Egypt.

Egypt now entered upon its first great period of history — the so-called Old Kingdom. Of all the royal families of that time, the fourth is perhaps the most interesting. It was this family that built the pyramids and brought Egypt to a peak of peace, power, and prosperity. The kings were Khufu (Cheops), Khafre, and Menkaure, and they ruled from 2680 to 2560 B.C.

The king of Egypt was usually called Pharaoh, which means the "Great House." Among his many titles was that of "King of Upper and Lower Egypt." As a sign that he was ruler of both kingdoms, he wore two crowns.

The Egyptian Pharaoh had almost unlimited powers. Not only was he head of the state religion and commander of the army, but he also administered justice — at least through his representatives.

The Pharaoh's right-hand man was the vizier, who helped him govern Egypt. The vizier was often the Pharaoh's own son, the crown prince. The nobles, the governors of the provinces, and other officials also helped their king govern the country.

In time, the people of Egypt came to believe that their Pharaoh was a god. They claimed that he was the son of Re, the sun god, and looked on him as Horus, the god of light.

Work and Trade

IN ORDER to raise as much food as possible, the Pharaoh decided each year which crops were to be planted, and in what quantities. The small farmer had less and less to say about his own farm. Finally he became a serf — a free man, but bound to the soil. Moreover, the Pharaoh actually owned all the land of Egypt and rented it to the people. The only important exceptions were the acres he gave to temples and priests, who thus became richer and richer.

The farmer paid his rent and taxes with the products of his farm. He also had to put in a number of days a year on the irrigation works, or in the mines and quarries, or in the shops that manufactured bricks.

There were neither camels nor horses in Egypt at the time of the Old Kingdom, but all sorts of other animals could be seen in the countryside. There were donkeys, pigs, oxen, sheep, goats, ducks, and geese. Date palms, pomegranate, olive, and fig trees grew in the fields. There were beautiful flower gardens. Since the Egyptians used honey for sweetening, most Egyptians kept bees.

An Egyptian farmer plowed his land with a wooden plow that looked very much like a hoe with a long handle pointing forward. He cultivated his crops with wooden hoes and rakes. He planted his land to beans and other vegetables, to barley and wheat, to flax for its linen, and to sesame plants for their fats. Animals were driven over the ground to trample in the seeds. When

An Egyptian farmer plowing

the grain was ripe, the farmer cut it with a bronze sickle, and threshed it by driving his cattle over it. Finally, he threw it into the wind to separate the grain from the chaff.

There was no coined money in Egypt, so when a man went shopping he traded a certain amount of grain, for example, for a cow or a bed. This is called barter.

Egyptian traders went to Nubia, to Phoenicia and Syria, to Asia Minor and the islands of the Aegean Sea. They brought back spices and incense, ebony, ivory, and gold. From the nearby Sinai Peninsula they obtained copper. Egypt had plenty of stone for building, but there were few trees for wood. For that reason the Egyptian traders traveled to Syria to barter for the famous "cedars of Lebanon," which they brought back to Egypt on barges.

11

Egyptian vases

In exchange for these things, the Egyptians exported beautiful jewelry of gold, silver, and copper; thin, nearly-transparent stone vases; exquisite furniture; fine linen tapestries. The craftsmen of ancient Egypt rank with the very best in history.

Egypt's great prosperity was partly due to the fact that nature gave her protection against foreign enemies. To the east was the Red Sea; to the west, the Sahara Desert; to the south, Nubia (modern Sudan), and tropical jungles; to the north, the Mediterranean Sea. Then, too, Egypt was a narrow, compact land, and the very flatness of the country, the ease of travel along the river, made it possible for her rulers to keep in touch with everything that was going on and thus develop a strong central government.

It was trade, however, that brought new ideas to Egypt and speeded the growth of her civilization. For example, when the Egyptians went to Syria for wood, they learned about astronomy and law, which had actually begun in Mesopotamia. Nothing helps a civilization to develop more rapidly than contact with important new ideas and customs.

12

Daily Life

THE UPPER CLASS of Egyptian society was made up of government officials, the nobles, and the priests. In the middle class were skilled workmen and artists, and other city dwellers who frequently engaged in trade. The largest class was the farming population, and at the bottom of the social scale were the slaves.

The Pharaoh lived in a luxurious palace at Memphis. Nearby were temples and official buildings, and the houses of the nobles. This was the fashionable part of town, but the houses were not as large as we might expect. This was because Memphis, like all other Egyptian cities, was built near the river, the chief means of

House of a wealthy Egyptian

travel and communication. Since only the land near the river was fit for civilization, as much of it as possible had to be used for farming. Living space was limited.

Town houses faced directly on the street and had very small gardens in the back. A noble's house usually rose two or three stories and was made of sun-dried mud brick. The family slept in an upper story at the back of the house, where it was quiet, while the slaves slept on the ground floor next to the noisy street. These town houses were quite modern in appearance.

The large country house of an Egyptian noble was a different thing entirely. It belonged clearly to a very wealthy man. It was on one floor, with courts and porches overlooking shady gardens, and pools full of lilies and fish. The slaves lived in a separate building to the rear. A wall, surrounding the entire property, assured the owner of privacy.

Egyptian country houses were furnished with some of the most splendid furniture ever known. Not only rare woods, such as ebony, but silver and other metals, and ivory went into its making. There were folding stools, chairs, and tables. To light the rooms at night there were cups, or dishes, filled with olive oil in which floated burning wicks. Beds were generally higher at the head than at the foot, and cushions often served as pillows. Strands of cord were used for bedsprings, and over these were stretched linen sheets to serve as mattresses.

The slaves cooked their masters' dinners in the slave quarters. They had fires of wood or charcoal, and used kettles and other

Ancient Egyptian furniture

cooking utensils much like those we use today. When the nobles sat down to dinner they ate from dishes of pottery and glass, of alabaster, and even of gold and other metals. Their meals were large and varied. They dined on milk and bread, fish, poultry, meat, vegetables, fruit, and honey in place of sugar.

Both men and women of the nobility wore wigs and jewelry and used cosmetics. The men shaved with bronze razors. They wore linen skirts and, unless they left the upper parts of their bodies bare, shirts of the same material. The women wore long linen dresses, and both sexes wore sandals.

The wife of a noble saw to it that her name was written in ink on her linens. She kept other valuables in sealed jars, baskets, and chests. The seal would not keep a thief out, but if it was broken, she would know that something had been stolen.

The Egyptians, whether rich or poor, seem to have had an exceptionally happy home life. With the exception of the Pharaoh, a man was allowed only one wife at a time. Sometimes, in a very rich family, a brother and sister married in order to keep the property in the family.

Egyptian children played with all sorts of toys — dogs with movable jaws, dolls, rattles, make-believe axes, and so on, very much as children do today. They ran and jumped and played games, while the grownups enjoyed bullfights or threw knuckle bones (in place of dice), and moved "men" over a board marked with squares like those on a chess or checkerboard.

Magicians, storytellers, dancers, and musicians provided entertainment for the whole family. The Egyptians were very fond of music. Not only professionals but amateurs played harps, lutes and flutes, oboes and clarinets.

One of the things that brings the Egyptians of ancient times closest to us today is their love of pets. They kept not only cats and dogs, but monkeys and gazelles.

The favorite sports of the Egyptians were fishing and hunting. These often provided food as well as pleasure. The Egyptians fished from the banks of the Nile, or from canoes, using nets, hooks, and spears.

The Egyptians also enjoyed trapping birds, or bringing them down with boomerangs. Cats were used to retrieve the game, just as dogs are used today. When a hunter set off for bigger game, such as wild cattle, hyenas, and the lions and elephants that lived

16

Hippopotamus hunt on the Nile. (Wall sculpture from the tomb of a pharaoh of the fifth dynasty.)

in the desert, he carried spears and bows and arrows and brought along several good hunting dogs.

Right beside the Nile itself the Egyptians hunted hippopotamuses and crocodiles. Herodotus, a Greek historian of the fifth century B.C. who visited Egypt, tells us that the commonest way of hunting crocodiles was as follows: "The Egyptians bait a hook with a cut of pork and let it float out into the middle of the river. The hunter sits on the bank and beats a living pig. The crocodile hears its cries and going in the direction of the noise, meets the pork and immediately swallows it. The men on shore pull in the line, and when they have landed the crocodile, the first thing they do is plaster its eyes with mud. Then they kill the animal easily; otherwise it gives much trouble."

17

Egyptian parents took special pains to teach both boys and girls good manners, but when it came to formal education, they favored the boys. The highest purpose of education was to prepare a boy for a post in the government. If a boy's ambition was a little lower, he might hope to become a scribe — an official clerk, or writer. Scribes were important members of the Egyptian middle class and often acted as teachers.

Whatever his aim in life, the first thing a boy learned was to read and write. He memorized proverbs, which were supposed to help him grow up, and practiced writing model letters such as he might have to use later on. Then he learned arithmetic and geometry. Mathematics was necessary because he might get a job keeping tax lists, and every imaginable thing was taxed to support the government. Or he might get a job of surveying and recording land and boundaries after the overflow of the Nile had swept away the landmarks of the year before.

An educated Egyptian could rise from a lower class to a higher. This was a healthy thing for the country because it brought new life and ideas to a society that might otherwise have gone along in the same old rut forever.

The life of the poor was in sharp contrast to the luxurious life of the nobles. Poor Egyptians lived in mud huts that were crowded close together along narrow, crooked lanes. Their clothing consisted of a single linen garment, and their food was simple.

The mother of the family was respected. She looked after the children, fetched water from the well or the river, ground meal between two stones, baked bread in the ashes of a wood fire, sewed, spun thread, and wove cloth.

The father's day was spent in the field or at his job. If he had a job as a carpenter, he used tools much like our own — mallets, axes, knives, chisels, and saws. His master could, and often did, beat him on the slightest excuse.

The poor people served in the army, but all the officers came from the nobility and the commercial middle class of the cities.

One thing all Egyptians, rich and poor, had in common was a lively imagination. They also had a sense of humor, were obedient to their superiors, and revered their god-king.

Religion

BECAUSE the land of Egypt was so flat, the scene was always the same no matter where a man looked. Always he saw the river and the green fields stretching away to the desert and the hills. But sometimes he would see an animal sunning itself on the flat plain. The animal appeared, by contrast, to have an extraordinary amount of life. And so it came about that the people of ancient Egypt thought of animals and other living, moving things as having souls, and even sometimes as gods.

The Egyptians believed in a number of good and evil spirits, which might dwell in a mountain or a tree, a star, or the moon or sun. The more powerful spirits, such as those of the moon or the sun, were looked upon as gods. In their painting and sculpture the Egyptians gave these spirits the forms of men and women, or of birds, crocodiles, jackals, cattle, cats, or dogs.

Some of the gods were worshiped by the whole population. Among these were Horus, the god of light, Re, the sun god, and Nut, goddess of the sky. Other gods, however, were purely local, and were worshiped in various villages.

The festivals in honor of the gods provided wonderful holidays for the people. There were plays telling the story of the god who was being honored. The plays told how the god had suffered and then at last had overcome his enemies and misfortunes. A figure of the god in a holy boat would be carried in procession by the priests, to the accompaniment of music and dancing.

Although all life in Egypt depended on the Nile, the Egyptians believed that the sun was the true source of life. When the sun disappeared in the evening, it suggested death. When it rose again in the morning, it suggested rebirth and a new life. The Nile, too, suggested rebirth, for every year it renewed life with its overflow. This influenced the Egyptians in one of their strongest beliefs — that when they died they would be reborn.

The king of the dead and immortality, or everlasting life, was Osiris. He sat at the judgment seat with his wife-sister, Isis, to decide whether a spirit entering the next world had belonged in life to a good person or a bad one. If the spirit was judged to have belonged to a good person, it would be given eternal happiness. If its owner had been bad, it would be turned over to a monster to

Tutenkhamon portrayed as Horus, god of light

be devoured. For this reason, the Egyptians spent a large part of their time preparing their souls for the next world. And if a man was rich and powerful he had still another reason for wanting to prepare for the next world — he found life on earth so delightful that he wanted to prolong it after death.

The Egyptians believed that the tomb, or burial place, served as a kind of bridge between life and death. Therefore they stored food and drink in it to keep the spirit alive. They painted cheerful pictures of daily life on the walls, and these pictures had to include food and drink so that the spirit would not have to leave the tomb when it had eaten all the real provisions.

Because the Egyptians thought the soul lived on in the body after death, they believed they must preserve the body as long as possible. The dry climate of Egypt helped, but not indefinitely. To preserve dead bodies as long as possible, the Egyptians embalmed, or mummified, them.

Herodotus, the historian of ancient Greece, described the best way to do this. "First," he wrote, "the Egyptians take a crooked piece of iron and draw the brains out through the nostrils, thus getting rid of some of it, while the skull is cleared of the rest by rinsing with drugs. Then they make an incision in the flank with a sharp stone and take out the entrails. Next, they cleanse the body and wash it with palm-wine. After this, they fill the body with myrrh, with cassia, and every other sort of spice, except frankincense, and sew up the opening.

"Then the body is soaked in saltpeter for forty days. The body is next washed once more and wrapped round with strips of fine linen. This is smeared over with gum. In this state the body is given back to the relatives, who enclose it in a wooden case, which they have made for the purpose, shaped in the figure of a man. Then fastening the case, they place it in the tomb, upright against the wall."

Poor people were buried quite simply, but the nobles were laid to rest in large, rectangular tombs of stone called mastabas. These clustered about the pyramids of the king, so that the nobles might continue to serve him in death and share in his immortality.

Tombs clustered around the pyramid of an Egyptian pharaoh

A King's Tomb Is Opened

In 1922 the English archaeologist, Howard Carter, found the tomb of a Pharaoh who ruled Egypt during the fourteenth century b.c. This in itself was not unusual. Such tombs had been discovered before. What made Carter's discovery important was that this tomb, unlike so many others, had not been opened by thieves and robbed of the treasures placed in it for the king's use in the next world. Carter's discovery not only tells us what the untouched tomb of a Pharaoh looks like, but it also emphasizes for us the dramatic way in which archaeology adds to our knowledge of the past.

For six years Carter had been excavating in the Valley of the Kings, to the west of Thebes. Many tombs had already been found there and excavated. Carter had covered every inch of the ground during those six years, thinking he might find the entrance to a tomb. He was about ready to give up and leave when a worker's hoe struck a sealed doorway.

The seals imprinted on the doorway, said Carter, were those of Tutenkhamon, who reigned from 1352 to 1344 b.c. In his excitement, Carter first made a little hole in the door and peeped through. With the help of a flashlight, he could see a passage filled with rubble, but nothing else. He re-covered the doorway, set men on guard for the night, and went back to his camp to sleep.

Finally the work began. Passages, stairways, and sealed doorways were opened and cleared until at last the diggers came to

(Right) Tutenkhamon

(Below) Shrine-shaped chest, overlaid with gold, found in Tutenkhamon's tomb

25

what seemed to be the final chamber. A small hole was made in the door, and one of the workmen held a lighted candle in front of it. But instead of the foul gases that were expected, hot air rushed out of the hole. When Carter took a look, he could see nothing at first except gold. Gold was everywhere. Then slowly Carter made out the forms of animals and statues, couches, beautiful alabaster vases, chairs, chariots, golden bouquets of flowers, and a throne. The throne was covered with sheet gold and decorated with glass of many colors, earthenware, and stone inlay.

One thing, however, Carter did not see. That was a mummy or a coffin. He began to realize that this was merely an antechamber, and that the greatest discoveries still lay ahead.

The work continued until the burial chamber itself was reached, and Carter drew back the bolts of the door. There, filling the room, was a huge sculptured sarcophagus, or coffin, of yellow

The sarcophagus of Harmhab, first pharaoh of the nineteenth dynasty

quartzite (rock composed of quartz). The lid was still on it.

The diggers had to bring in block and tackle to raise the lid, for it weighed over a ton and a quarter. Inside they found a whole nest of coffins, one inside the other. The lid of the first was a golden representation of the young king. But amid all this splendor and wealth, the thing that touched Carter most deeply was a tiny wreath of flowers left there, no doubt, by Tutenkhamon's young, widowed queen.

Tutenkhamon's body had been carefully mummified and wrapped in fine linen. But so many unguents had been poured on it during the last ceremony of anointing that the body had decomposed much more than those of most Egyptian mummies.

The Pyramids

THE PHARAOHS of the fourth dynasty (2680-2560 B.C.) built tremendous burial structures for themselves. These pyramids, as we call them, stand on the edge of the desert not far from Memphis, to the west of the Nile, at modern Gizeh. The largest one, that of King Khufu (Cheops), covers thirteen acres. It took a hundred thousand men to build it, and the work went on for twenty years. Two and a half million blocks of stone were used, and each block weighed about two and a half tons. That makes six and a quarter million tons of stone. The total tonnage of New York's Empire State Building is about three hundred thousand.

The building of the great pyramid, as it might have been seen from the air

The pyramid at Gizeh represents one of the most amazing architectural and engineering feats in the whole history of the human race. Since iron was unknown at the time, the Egyptians had to use tools of stone, copper, and bronze. The block and tackle had not been invented, so the great blocks of stone had to be lifted into place by means of ropes, levers, and rollers manned by tens of thousands of slaves.

No one has yet discovered all the details of the building of this great pyramid, but we have a clear enough general picture of how it was done. The Pharaoh chose a place for his pyramid on the edge of the desert, but beyond the harmful reach of the Nile's overflow. Then a great many limestone blocks were quarried east of the Nile and ferried across the river. The Egyptians did this when the river's overflow was at its height so that the rafts could come as close as possible to the site of the pyramid.

Slaves then unloaded the blocks and dragged them on rollers along a stone causeway, or road, that had been built right up to where the pyramid was to stand.

The site chosen for the pyramid was solid rock. This was leveled off, and then the work was started. The base of the pyramid was 755 feet on each side. The mass of stone blocks that now went into the construction of the great burial place were quarried nearby. As the pyramid rose, mud brick ramps were built against its sides so that more and more blocks could be rolled up into place. The pyramid was actually built in a series of steps, and it grew narrower as it rose. There are 137 steps, or courses, as they are called. The total height of Khufu's pyramid is 481 feet.

Once the courses had been laid, the Egyptians faced the great structure with the white limestone blocks they had ferried across the Nile. The pyramid was now absolutely smooth from top to bottom. The blocks of limestone fitted to a fiftieth of an inch. There was no need to secure them with mortar, with precision such as this. Most of these blocks were stolen by looters in later ages. That is why the pyramid today has its stepped appearance.

The Pharaoh was especially anxious that robbers should not find his actual tomb, so it was placed far inside the pyramid. From a hidden door on the north side, a 156-foot passageway goes down, then winds upward to the king's tomb. On the way it passes the the queen's tomb and various chapels for the worship of the royal pair's spirits.

When the time came to close up the pyramid, the doors of the king's and queen's tombs were sealed, and huge blocks were rolled into the passageway. Nevertheless, in later times robbers did get in and steal the contents of the tombs. The most important thing they left behind was the plain, granite sarcophagus that originally held Khufu's body. It was too big to carry away.

Near this great pyramid stood temples and the mastabas of the nobles. The other kings of the fourth dynasty, Khafre and Menkaure, also built their pyramids here. Just as Khufu did, they built them during their lifetime because they were unwilling to trust anyone else to attend to their souls' resting places.

The sphinx at Gizeh

It was Khafre who built the famous Sphinx beside his pyramid. The head of the Sphinx is a portrait of himself, 66 feet high, but the body is that of a lion to suggest the king's great strength and power.

By building these huge structures the Pharaohs of the fourth dynasty used up endless natural resources, to say nothing of the thousands of human lives they sacrificed. None of the kings who came later could match them. In his description of the pyramids Herodotus says: "There is an inscription in Egyptian characters on the pyramid that gives the amount of radishes, onions, and garlic used by the laborers. I remember the interpreter who translated for me, saying that the money spent in this way was 1,600 talents of silver (1 talent = $1,800). If this is correct, what a huge amount must have gone for the tools and for the feeding and clothing of the workers."

31

Art

EGYPTIAN art is full of life, with a wonderful sense of proportion and balance. From the wall paintings of the tombs and temples we get a realistic picture of how the Egyptians once lived.

Egyptian sculptures have great power. They are done in wood, copper, bronze, gold, and stone. The Egyptians were excellent portrait artists, too.

Egyptian paintings were done in bright colors. They illustrate for us almost all the activities of these people of ancient times — feasting, dancing, work in the fields, and so on. Moreover, they tell us important things about the Egyptians — that they loved life and material things, and that they were gay and merry.

Since so much of the art was connected with religion — with temples and tombs — the Egyptians felt that they must not change its style from generation to generation. They did not experiment with new ideas. In painting, for example, a man's eye is always shown in full view, even when the face is shown in profile. In sculpture, men were carved facing forward, arms to the side, with one leg a little ahead of the other. But the really important thing about Egyptian painting and sculpture is that it was always a thing of fine taste. This is true of whatever the Egyptians made, whether it was jewelry, furniture, or any other decorative art.

The grandeur of Egyptian architecture is to be seen not only in the pyramids, but in the stone temples as well. A typical Egyptian temple was generally entered through two outer courts whose gates

"The Water Carrier," early Egyptian sculpture, and wall paintings

33

Temple at Karnak

were flanked by twin towers. These towers were called the *pylon*. Then came several halls filled with huge columns. Beyond was the great central, columned hall, known as the *hypostyle*. The uppermost part of its columns — the capitals — were likely to represent papyrus flowers.

The center of the hypostyle was higher than its side aisles. This arrangement allowed light to come in by windows in the walls, and was called a *clerestory*. Back of the hypostyle was the sanctuary of the god of the temple.

Carved and painted on the walls of the temple were pictures of most of the great deeds of the Pharaoh who had built it. Still more of his deeds were carved on the four-sided, tapering pillars, known as *obelisks,* that stood outside.

Science and Literature

THE EGYPTIANS were a practical people, and to them knowledge was important chiefly when it was useful. They learned arithmetic, geometry, and surveying because property boundaries had to be relocated each year after the Nile's overflow. A knowledge of engineering was necessary for the building of the pyramids. Religion, and the need for arranging a calendar of festivals, encouraged their interest in astronomy.

The Egyptian year began on what is about July 19 by our calendar. That is when the Nile begins to rise. Astronomers noticed that this came at almost the exact time the Dog Star, Sirius, rose with the sun. By counting the number of days until the Dog Star once more rose at dawn, they worked out a calendar of 365 days. It was a very remarkable accomplishment, although the absence of an extra day every fourth year upset certain festivals. This was corrected by adding extra days to the year every so often.

Egyptians made important beginnings in the study of anatomy and physiology, too. They were the first to discover that the pulse had something to do with the heart's beat. According to their thinking, the blood ran from the heart to the eyes, ears, and nose. The Egyptians also learned how to make splints for broken bones. Unfortunately, however, the study of medicine was held back by superstition and the Egyptians' belief in magic. They thought that evil spirits caused disease. Sometimes they used herbs and drugs to cure people, and sometimes these things worked. But more generally a priest tried to drive out a disease by reciting certain words or phrases, which he might then write down and tie around the neck of the sick person.

Egyptian literature had great dignity, but like Egyptian science, its chief aim was to be useful. For example, an author might tell his reader what to do when he died, so that he would win immortality. Another might write directions on how to get along in this life. An Egyptian book of etiquette advises the reader to become an official and to learn the rules, and to treat his superiors, equals, and inferiors fairly.

Rosetta Stone

The Rosetta Stone

WE WOULD know nothing about Egyptian literature if we could not read the strange Egyptian writing. The secret was cracked only in the last century. The story begins in 1799 with the discovery of a piece of black basalt stone, three feet nine inches long, two feet four inches wide, and eleven inches thick. Since it was found near the Rosetta branch of the Nile, it has been called the Rosetta Stone ever since. Today it is in the famous British Museum in London.

The front side of the Rosetta Stone consists of three panels covered with writing. The bottom panel is written in Greek, which

37

scholars could read at once. The top panel is written in the priestly form of Egyptian writing, the picture writing called *hieroglyphics*. In the center is a simpler form of writing — called *demotic,* the people's writing — which could be read by ordinary Egyptians.

Scholars saw that the Greek text could prove to be the key to the Egyptian writing. A Frenchman, Jean François Champollion, noticed that the panel with the hieroglyphics contained five ovals, or *cartouches,* as they are called. Then he noticed that the Greek text mentioned the king's name five times. He made the good guess that the cartouches contained the king's name. In this way he was able to put one of our letters opposite each of the Egyptian signs.

This same thing was done over and over on other Egyptian monuments until, after many years' brilliant labor, the entire Egyptian language had been *transliterated* — that is, we could supply one of our letters for each of their signs. The Egyptian language could at least be pronounced. *Translation,* putting the words into another language, was another matter, but it proved to be easy.

It so happens that a knowledge of ancient Egyptian has never been lost. When St. Mark preached in Alexandria and converted many Egyptians to Christianity, the Bible was written out in Greek letters for the converts. The language was actually the old Egyptian language, but the Christian form of it is called *Coptic.*

Champollion had mastered many languages as a young man, including Coptic. When he had put one of our letters after each hieroglyphic sign on the Rosetta Stone, he saw at once that the language was Coptic. He read it right off, and his translation was just like the Greek text in the bottom panel. It is in this way that the whole world of ancient Egyptian writing has been opened up for us.

The Middle Kingdom (2000-1785 B.C.)

THE POWER of the Egyptian nobles increased steadily through the centuries. In fact, the nobles became so strong that they began to express their own ideas about government and religion and art, each in his own particular way. As a result of this, the Pharaoh lost a good deal of the power and authority he had in the past. At the same time, Negroes, Libyans, and Semites began to invade the country. In 2280 B.C., the Old Kingdom fell.

Until 2000 B.C. Egypt was torn by civil wars. Then some powerful Egyptians in Thebes drove out the foreigners and united Egypt once again. It was in this way that the Middle Kingdom began. Thebes was the new capital.

The nobles kept a good deal of power at first. They had vast estates with many serfs. But most Egyptians realized that the strong, central government of the Old Kingdom had prevented civil war and foreign invasion, and so they accepted powerful rulers again.

Amenemhet III, a king of the twelfth dynasty, ruled with abso-

39

lute power, but he brought back peace and prosperity to Egypt. He sent his agents, known as "the Eyes and Ears of the King," throughout the kingdom. They watched and listened, and reported back to the king what the people were doing and thinking. They let him know whether the people were hard at work, or whether they were dissatisfied and perhaps plotting against their ruler. One thing in particular these agents did, and that was to make sure that the provincial governors sent the king his share of the taxes promptly.

To encourage trade, Amenemhet III had a canal dug around the first cataract of the Nile at Syene, where it was impossible for ships to navigate. He had another canal dug from the east branch

Egyptian trading vessel

of the Nile to the Red Sea. Trade with Punt (now Somaliland), with Syria, Cyprus, and Crete was lively and profitable. Egypt conquered Nubia and turned it into a province.

Egypt became so powerful and prosperous under the twelfth dynasty that she was able to increase her farm lands by adding thousands of acres in an oasis just west of the Nile and south of Memphis. Today this area is known as the Fayum. Each year the overflow of the Nile passed through a natural cut in the hills into the Fayum, but the water receded as the river fell. The kings of the twelfth dynasty decided to save this water. They built dams and canals so that some of the water could be saved to irrigate the Fayum. The rest they released during the driest months for use farther down along the Nile.

Religion

DURING the Old Kingdom the dead Pharaoh became Osiris, king of the dead. But since the Pharaohs of the Middle Kingdom did not completely destroy the power of the nobles, the nobles and even the poor people began to claim some of the king's privileges. They, too, became kings of the dead when they died, and were allowed to hope for immortality.

One privilege, however, the kings of the twelfth dynasty kept for themselves. They had as their own patron god the ram-headed god of Thebes called Amon. They now joined Amon to the old

41

national god, Re. Amon-Re, they decreed, was to be the chief god of Egypt.

The religion of the Middle Kingdom placed great emphasis on justice, honor, and purity. People wanted to be approved not only by the gods, but by their neighbors. Most of them hoped to be remembered as honest men who had obeyed the laws of the gods and their country.

Art and Literature

PYRAMIDS were still built during the Middle Kingdom, but their workmanship did not equal the splendor of those of the Old Kingdom. The tombs of the nobles no longer clustered about the Pharaoh's pyramid in the hope of sharing his immortality. To show their independence, the nobles cut their tombs in the cliffs along the west side of the Nile, at Abydos. This was a short distance down the river from Thebes.

The paintings continued to stress merrymaking, banquets, dancing, and music. Many showed Egyptians hunting with their dogs, or at work in the fields.

The best work of this time, however, was produced by the sculptors. They had learned to carve the muscles and flesh and blood vessels of a man with great skill. What was even more important, they had learned how to express a person's character.

In the Metropolitan Museum of Art in New York City there is

Necklace from the fifth dynasty. This is in the Metropolitan Museum of Art in New York City.

a marvelous necklace that proves that the Egyptian craftsmen of the Middle Kingdom were as gifted as those before them. The necklace is of gold, carnelian, and green feldspar. It belonged to a daughter of Sesostris II, a king of the twelfth dynasty.

The literature of the Middle Kingdom, like the religion, stressed justice, purity, and honesty. The writers said that all good things were available to all men, and that it was just as possible for the poor as for the rich, for the common people as for the nobles, to live good lives. Never before in history had people set themselves such high standards of conduct. Never before had they said that ordinary people were as good and fine as the well born.

Much of Egyptian literature contained religious texts and magic spells. These were brought together in an extraordinary collection known as *The Book of the Dead*. All sorts of strange things can be found in this book. It describes the next world, and warns of the monsters the dead may meet there. It also tells the reader how he can take this or that shape after he has died. The book has religious poems and hymns to the gods, too.

Other forms of Egyptian literature consisted of love songs, and the simple songs of shepherds and laborers. There were also historical accounts, and stories of travel and adventure. One story of adventure tells about a sailor who was shipwrecked in the Red Sea and, after many adventures, returned home joyously at last. It reminds one of the tales of Sinbad.

The New Kingdom (1580-1085 B.C.)

IN 1785 B.C., at a time of weak rulers and foreign invasion, the Middle Kingdom fell. The invaders were a Semitic people from Asia known as the Hyksos, who introduced horses and war chariots to Egypt. Two centuries later, a remarkable Egyptian general of Thebes, Ahmose by name, reunited the country, became its ruler, and drove out the Hyksos. This was the beginning of the New Kingdom, or Empire (1580 B.C.), when the eighteenth, nineteenth, and twentieth dynasties ruled Egypt. The capital remained at Thebes.

The Egyptians had been through such a long and terrible time with the Hyksos that they now wanted security above everything else. Loyalty to Egypt was demanded of everyone. No longer were people allowed to speak their minds freely and openly about government, religion, art, or anything else. No longer was it important for a man to be himself. Everybody was busy trying to be like everybody else. The large and growing army influenced not only government policies, but also the lives and thoughts of the people. Egypt's frontiers, people said, must be extended as far as possible so that no enemy could ever again invade the country.

The Pharaoh was once more the divine and absolute ruler, the owner of all the land. His chief support came from the priests, to whom he gave richer and richer gifts. A tremendous governmental machinery, or bureaucracy, was developed to manage and direct the fifty-five provinces and the collection of the crushing taxes.

Thutmose I, who ruled after Ahmose, chose a new burial ground for himself in a valley to the west of Thebes. So many Pharaohs were later buried there that it came to be known as the "Valley of the Kings." Thutmose did not want robbers to enter his tomb, and thought that he had chosen a place that would always remain a secret. He was mistaken about the region remaining a secret, but it has not always been easy to discover the actual tombs, as Howard Carter learned!

Another Thutmose, the third of that name, was a gifted general. There is a wonderful portrait of him in the Cairo Museum that brings out his strength of character. Thutmose III led over twenty military expeditions, chiefly against Syria. In 1479 B.C. at

Thutmose III

Megiddo, the Armageddon of the Bible, he won an important victory over his enemy, the king of Kadesh. He followed this up with a victory at Carchemish on the Euphrates. Now the Egyptian Empire extended from Mesopotamia to the Nile. The mighty Pharaoh could count on a rich tribute of slaves and horses, gold, silver, and timber.

The last and most magnificent ruler of the great eighteenth dynasty was Amenhotep III (1411-1375 B.C.). Egypt was now the most powerful state on earth. Princes from various parts of the empire were brought to Egypt and educated. Then they went home to their provinces to rule as servants of the Pharaoh. Ties with other countries were strengthened and peace was insured by the Pharaoh's habit of marrying native princesses. The laws that forbade a man more than one wife did not apply to the Pharaoh.

In spite of all this, however, there were troubles in the empire. The rich were growing richer, the poor, poorer. The captives, brought from conquered lands to work for Egypt, were restless.

Several hundred interesting letters addressed to Amenhotep have been discovered at a place that today is called Tell el-Amarna. They are all from foreign states and are written on clay tablets. We do not have the Pharaoh's replies, but they were probably written on papyri. The letters give us a vivid glimpse of the peoples that made up Amenhotep's world. The diplomatic correspondence has to do with the Babylonians and Assyrians, the Hittites of Asia Minor, the people of Cyprus, and the Minoans of Crete, who are spoken of as living on the Isles of the Sea. It was a large and civilized world and its products, from Greece to Nubia and Punt, poured into Egypt.

Art and Religion

EGYPTIAN sculptors continued to turn out excellent portraits and some amusing caricatures as well. But the country's great prosperity, and its emphasis on material things gradually affected life in general. For example, the clothes and jewelry of the Egyptians, their houses and furniture, were pretty much the same as before, except that everything was more magnificent and expensive. When the architects built palaces and temples they were more concerned with size than beauty. The buildings in the towns of Karnak and Luxor were especially huge. These two places were a mile and a half apart, and were connected by a straight avenue lined, on either side, with stone statues of rams. Even today it is a spectacular sight. Another extraordinary sight is the temple Amenhotep built at Luxor for the worship of his spirit. In front of it are two stone statues of the Pharaoh, each one weighing 700 tons.

Religion, like literature and art, remained very much as it had been. People were satisfied with things as they were, and did not want to change them. They did not welcome new ideas, nor new ways of doing things. They still went through the form of wor-

Ship of the Dead. (Model found in an Egyptian tomb.)

shiping Isis, Osiris, and Horus, but they were inclined to forget the old emphasis on right thinking and doing.

It was easy for people to look in *The Book of the Dead* and find convenient little formulas by which to escape punishment when Osiris was judging them. And just in case any work might be required of them after they died, small figurines, known as "Answers," were buried with them to do the work.

The paintings on the walls of tombs still showed scenes from daily life. A typical painting, done in the usual bright colors, showed a noble sitting in a booth overlooking his fields. Girls are winnowing the grain and wearing kerchiefs to protect their hair from the fine dust. The men are measuring the grain under the direction of an overseer.

Most of the paintings, however, no longer emphasized the joy and richness of life. They pictured death, resignation, and the hope of a better life in the next world. These paintings tell us that at a time when a man was no longer allowed to think, speak, and act for himself he was left with little more than the hope of better things after death.

Queen Tiy, the wife of Amenhotep III, was one of the common people, and perhaps strange ideas were to be expected of their son. At any rate, when the son came to the throne as Amenhotep IV, he soon introduced ideas that changed the thinking of many of his people.

The young Pharaoh thought it wrong that the government should have such complete control over the lives of the people.

Akhnaton

Furthermore, he thought it wrong that the priests should have so much power that they could tell people exactly what they must think and believe.

Amenhotep IV looked at the vast Egyptian Empire that stretched from Mesopotamia to the Nile. It was inhabited by many different kinds of people, but when you looked at them closely,

Nofretete

one was very much like another. Amenhotep IV had the feeling that the whole world was inhabited by people who were pretty much the same everywhere. And this made him think about a god who would be the same for all men, everywhere.

As Amenhotep IV thought about one god, it occurred to him that the one thing that affected all men alike was the life-giving sun. So he adopted Aton for his god, because the Egyptian symbol for Aton was the sun disk.

Immediately Amenhotep IV set out to destroy the religion of the old god, Amon, and his priests. He even changed his name to Akhnaton, which means "Aton be pleased."

The priests of Amon and the masses of the people strongly disapproved of Akhnaton's new policy. He therefore moved his capital from Thebes, the center of the old religion, to a city that he called Akhetaton (the modern Tell el-Amarna).

The new religion brought new ideas to Egypt. With new ideas came a wonderful freedom of expression, particularly in the arts. Instead of portraying people in the old, formal style, artists now portrayed them in natural and lifelike poses.

One of the finest of all Egyptian portraits is a painted, limestone head of Akhnaton's wife, Nofretete, found at Tell el-Amarna. Today it is one of the greatest treasures of the Berlin Museum. In the famous Cairo Museum there is a beautiful limestone relief that shows Akhnaton and Nofretete together. They are worshiping the Sun Disk, symbol of their god, Aton.

Another treasure of the Berlin Museum is a wonderfully realistic portrait of Queen Tiy. It is of carved wood and stucco, with inlaid eyes and gold earrings. Tiy may have been a commoner, but her portrait suggests the sensitive and determined lady who busied herself helping her son carry out his religious reforms.

Akhnaton was so busy with these reforms that he did not notice how his greedy officials were oppressing the people. Moreover, the powerful Hittites of Asia Minor were expanding, and there were rumblings of war along Egypt's frontiers. When the great Pharaoh died, the Egyptians decided to reunite, to forget their differences, and to return to the ways of the past. The capital was changed back again to Thebes.

The priests of Amon had won the battle against those who wanted to bring new ideas to Egypt. Once more it was the style to think and act like everybody else.

Ramses II (1292-1225 B.C.)

THE RETURN to the ways of old did not solve Egypt's problems immediately. As a result, the government was so busy trying to bring about order inside the country that it neglected to guard the country's frontiers properly. The Libyans saw their chance, and invaded and overran the country. Finally Ramses I, the founder of the nineteenth dynasty, drove them out and restored order.

The long reign of his great and famous son, Ramses II, brought magnificence back to Egypt on a grand scale. It was a strange kind of magnificence, however, for it neither cared for nor understood good taste. All that mattered was size. Ramses II built a temple at Abu Simbel, far up the Nile, on either side of which he placed pairs of statues of himself that are sixty-five feet high.

Ramses was so conceited that he put his name on ancient statues, and at times even had their faces recarved to look like his own.

To make his buildings more magnificent, he sometimes carried away parts or furnishings of other buildings.

At Thebes, Ramses built an enormous temple known as the Ramesseum, 590 feet long by 180 feet wide. But this was nothing compared to the temple he built at Karnak. It is one of the largest buildings in the world, 1215 feet long and 376 feet wide. The columns of the central hall are so huge that a hundred men can stand on the top of one.

For all his faults, Ramses was a brave man. He led an army north in 1288 B.C. to win back Syria from the Hittites. At Kadesh, on the Orontes River, he was ambushed by the Hittites. He rallied his men with fierce courage and cut his way out. Though the battle was far from a victory, he proudly recorded it on the walls of various temples in Egypt.

Shortly after, Ramses and the Hittite king, Hattushil, drew up a treaty. Two copies of this treaty have been found in Egypt, and another among the ancient public records of the Hittite capital in Asia Minor. The document called thousands of gods to witness. It then divided Syria between the Egyptian and Hittite rulers, renewed previous treaties, and arranged for the two countries to defend each other in case of attack.

Perhaps the most interesting clause in the treaty is the one calling for the surrender by each state of the refugees of the other, and guaranteeing their decent treatment when they returned home. It emphasizes a humaneness we might not expect in that far-off time.

A pharaoh pursuing his enemies. (From a wall sculpture in an Egyptian temple.)

The Fall of Egypt

FOREIGN INVADERS again disturbed Egypt, but once again order was restored, this time by the twentieth dynasty. The last important Pharaoh was Ramses III, who reigned from 1198 to 1167 B.C. By this time, however, the Egyptians had lost the will to fight. They had given over the protection of their country to paid foreign soldiers, or mercenaries. Not only was this expensive, but it was also dangerous, for mercenaries cannot be depended upon in an emergency. Another terrible, and almost unbearable, expense was the support of the numberless priests, their many temples, and great tracts of land.

Added to these troubles inside the country, Egypt was again threatened on her frontiers. These were days of great tribal upheavals and migrations. Barbarians overwhelmed the Hittites. In the western corner of Asia Minor, Greeks battered at the walls of Troy. The Philistines occupied the coast of Palestine. And in 1085 B.C., Libyans and other foreigners seized Egypt. The New Kingdom, and with it Egypt's long and great period in history, came to an end.

The Legacy of Egypt

ONE of the most dramatic lessons of ancient Egypt is the amazingly long time that an autocratic state can last, even when faced by many enemies. Although the lives of the ordinary people were often difficult, they revered their ruler, whom they believed to be both human and divine. They felt that he guarded them against the injustices of officials, and took their parts in disputes with the gods.

The Pharaoh surrounded himself with so many officials and nobles that a large privileged class was developed and supported. As a result, many Egyptians, through many centuries, were able

*Pyramid
at Gizeh*

to spend most of their time in creative activities. The pyramids
may have been built at the cost of many lives, but the splendid
contents of the tombs — the furniture, sculptures, and wall paintings — show a degree of fine taste that has never been surpassed.
The temples and pyramids of the Egyptians are so huge that we
never cease to marvel at what men could do with primitive tools.

57

The sculpture of the Egyptians probably represents their highest achievement, although their science, religion, and literature command high respect.

The long history of Egypt also emphasizes what a deadening thing conservatism and convention can be. And then it shows how the human spirit can be suddenly released, as it was by the reforms of Akhnaton, and carried to new and unsuspected heights.

Egypt's long civilization helped waken the Greeks to their own great achievements. And its monuments still stand in the valley of the Nile, beckoning to us to examine their meaning.

Index

reflects daily life, 32, 42, 49
revival of, under Akhnaton, 52
Asia Minor, 11, 47, 53, 54, 56
Astronomy, 12, 35-36
Aswan, 1
Aton, god, 52

Book of the Dead, The, 44, 49
Burial, 22-23, 42

Cairo, 1
Calendar, 6, 35-36
Canals, 40-41
Carchemish, battle of, 46
Carter, Howard, 25, 45
Champollion, Jean François, 38-39
Cheops, King, 9, 27, 30
Civil wars, 39
Civilization:
    beginnings of, 2-4
    spreading of, from Egypt, 7
Classes, social, 13, 18, 19, 43
Clothing, 15, 18, 47
Coptic language, 38-39
Crafts, 4-5
    in Middle Kingdom, 43
    in Old Kingdom, 12
Crete, 41, 47
Cyprus, 41, 47

Dead, The Book of the, 44, 49
Death, life after, 20-22
Demotic writing, 38
Dynasties:
    eighteenth, 44-47
    fourth, 9, 27, 31
    nineteenth, 53
    twelfth, 39, 41, 43
    twentieth, 55

Education, 18

Egypt:
    beginning of civilization in, 2-8
    borders of, 12, 46, 54
    geographical features of, 1-2, 12
    invasions of, 39, 44, 53, 55
    Kingdoms of, 8
    legacy of, 56-58
    origin of people of, 7
    Upper *vs.* Lower, 1, 9
Eighteenth dynasty, 44-47
Entertainment, 16
Ethiopia, 1

Farming, 10-11
Fayum, 41
Fishing, 16
Food, 14-15, 18
Fourth dynasty, 9, 27, 31
Furniture, 12, 14, 32, 47, 57

Games, 16
Gizeh, 27, 29
Gods, 9, 19-20, 41-42, 49, 51-52, 56
    See also names of gods
Government:
    of Middle Kingdom, 39-40
    of New Kingdom, 44-45, 49, 53
    of Old Kingdom, 9, 12
Greece, 6, 7, 47, 56, 58

Hattushil, King of Hittites, 54
Herodotus, 17, 22, 31
Hieroglyphs, 5, 38
Hittites, 47, 53, 54, 56
Holidays, religious, 20
Home life:
    of poor, 16, 18-19
    of wealthy, 14-17
Horus, god of light, 9, 20, 49
Housing, 13-14, 47
    of the poor, 18